COMPOSTING FOR BEGINNERS

A Beginner Bible to Compost
Everything at Home

BY

BRAIN KEVIN

Contents

INTRODUCTION

Composting: What Is It?

Composting is a natural process that transforms organic waste, like leaves and food scraps, into a useful fertilizer that benefits both plants and soil. Composting merely expedites the decomposition process by creating the perfect habitat for bacteria, fungi, and other decomposing creatures (such as worms, sowbugs, and nematodes) to carry out their functions. Everything that develops eventually decomposes. Compost is the term used to describe the final decomposed material, which frequently looks like fertile garden soil. Compost, also referred to as "black gold" by farmers, is beneficial in agriculture, horticulture, and gardening since it is nutrient-rich.

Among other possibilities, organic waste can be handled in anaerobic digesters, community composting systems, and industrial-scale composting facilities. This manual primarily focuses on home composting, which is an excellent way to keep your organic waste out of the waste stream and create a useful soil amendment for your use.

CHAPTER 1

ADVANTAGES OF COMPOST

Decrease Waste Stream

We may recycle the organic waste we produce at home by composting. Together, food leftovers and garden waste account for more than 28% of what we discard. Food waste processing is expensive in addition to being a huge environmental burden. In 2019, the price per ton of landfill municipal solid trash in the US was approximately $55. We spent billions of dollars on waste management in 2017 when the United States produced more than 267 million tons of municipal waste and sent two-thirds of it to landfills and incinerators. We can prevent part of that trash from going to landfills by composting it at home, where it can be transformed into useful material for our gardens.

Reduces Methane Emissions from Landfills

Usually, when organic matter decomposes, it does so aerobically, which means that oxygen-dependent microorganisms break it down. Compostable waste that is disposed of in a landfill is buried behind a mountain of other garbage, preventing the decomposers' frequent access to oxygen. The trash is subsequently subjected to anaerobic decomposition, whereby organisms that can survive without oxygen-free air break down the waste. Biogas is created during the anaerobic breakdown process. This biogas is about 50 percent methane and 50 percent carbon dioxide, both potent greenhouse gases, with methane being 28 to 36 times more effective at keeping the

4

heat in the atmosphere than carbon dioxide for a century. Landfills are the third-largest source of human-generated methane emissions in the United States, even though most modern landfills include methane capture devices, these do not fully absorb the gas.

Because our solid waste infrastructure is designed around a landfill, only about 6 percent of food waste is composted. However, states, cities, individual companies, and suppliers can implement zero-waste strategies to increase composting and recycling rates within their jurisdictions and prevent waste from being produced in the first place.

Increases Soil Health and Reduces Erosion

The use of compost is crucial for enhancing industrial-scale agriculture systems. The three main nutrients nitrogen, phosphorous, and potassium are found in compost. Additionally, it contains minute amounts of other necessary substances like calcium, magnesium, iron, and zinc. Composting offers an organic substitute for synthetic fertilizers that are filled with dangerous chemicals. Compost has the potential to boost soil water retention, resilience, and productivity, according to research.

Saves Water

About 80% of the water used in the US is used by agriculture, making it a significant water consumer in the country. Even though irrigation systems are efficient, managing them costs farmers money and time. In addition, accessing water is getting more and more challenging nationwide.

How is compost useful? According to research, adding organic matter to soil improves its ability to hold water. Each 1% increase in soil organic matter increases the soil's capacity to hold water by 20,000 gallons per acre. In comparison to farming on deteriorated soil, utilizing compost to promote healthy soil allows farmers to use less water while yet producing higher yields.

Reduces the Waste of Household Food

A shocking amount of food is wasted as a result of consumer behavior. Approximately $150 worth of food is wasted each month by a typical American family of four, a 50% increase since the 1970s. According to NRDC studies conducted in three American cities, fruits and vegetables are the category of edible food that households waste the most. A 2016 article in The Guardian said that over 60 million tons, or

$160 billion, worth of produce, are thrown away each year by American consumers and retailers. The greatest way to lessen the effects of food waste is to avoid waste in the first place, therefore NRDC works to inform consumers on how to buy for, prepare, and store food to reduce waste through its **Save the Food campaign** and other resources. However, there will still be food leftovers that cannot be eaten even if we take every precaution to reduce food waste (e.g., a banana peel). Instead of throwing these waste materials in the trash, composting is a fantastic way to recycle them.

CHAPTER 2

COMPOSTING BASIS

Compost is a crucial tool for organic farmers and gardeners. Compost is made from organic wastes including kitchen scraps, paper, and yard clippings, therefore composting is an efficient approach to recycling waste materials while generating a useful byproduct that feeds plants for healthy growth. Compost is made from the aerobic digestion of materials normally considered waste.

Basics of Compost

Compost is prepared by handling aerobic decay of organic matter such as grass leaves, kitchen scraps, paper, manures, straw, hay, wood chips, and sawdust.

Complex communities of microorganisms feed on these inputs, destroy them and release valuable nutrients for the plant. When microorganisms feed the temperature of the pile will increase. When decomposition is at its most rapid, compost often reaches temperatures of 130°F or more. The temperature of the compost pile will drop to that of the surrounding air as additional material decomposes. The pile now cures and is prepared to be used as a soil supplement.

Compost Building Blocks

Composting needs four fundamental components:

1. Water: Water is essential to maintain microbial life in the lint.

2. Oxygen: Oxygen helps maintain aerobic conditions.

3. Nitrogen: Nitrogen-rich materials, commonly known as **"green,"** are often more humid and have a higher nitrogen-to-carbon ratio. Greens include things like grass, coffee grounds, and food scraps.

4. Carbon: Carbon-rich, or **"brown,"** materials balance green materials and are typically dry and brittle materials such as leaves, straw, newspapers, and wood chips.

What Can Be Composted and What Can't?

Yes

"Green"

1. Most food waste.

2. Ground coffee and filters.

3. Vegetables and fruits

4. Eggshell

5. Manures

6. Herb

"Brown"

1. Dirty tissues and paper plates.

2. Newspaper

3. Leaves and straw

4. Wood chips

5. Yard scraps

No

1. Plastic

2. Mirror

3. Metal

4. Styrofoam

5. Meat*

6. Milk*

7. Oily foods *

8. Fatty products *

Note: These resources can be composted. But they run the risk of attracting pests and causing odors if not handled properly. Compost only if you have experience.

System Selection

There are numerous ways to compost. All of the available bins and systems can be successful, yet they all have different costs and advantages.

An **open pile** is probably the most typical composting technique. This works provided you have some space and are not too close to any neighbors, as open piles are sometimes poorly managed and can attract pests and bad odors.

You can **construct your bin** using cinder blocks, wood pallets, chicken wire, welded wire, drums, and trash cans. Bins made of welded wire are the most economical. Additionally, you can **buy a pre-made bin** online or at your neighborhood gardening supply store.

Note: To improve airflow and drainage, elevate your bin on a wooden pallet or lay the bottom with stalky material.

Volume should be considered when selecting a bin. Something at least 3x3x3 feet in size is recommended. By doing this, the surface-to-volume ratio will be reduced and heat retention during composting will be improved.

Scraps Preparation for Piles

Keep a bowl in the kitchen to collect food scraps as soon as you make them. When the container is full, pour it into the compost pile. The size of the container will depend on your needs and the amount of waste you usually produce. Avoid sealing the container. This will cause anaerobic conditions leading to an unpleasant odor. Or partially cover the container or cover it with a cloth to prevent unpleasant odors and prevent fruit flies.

Cutting, chopping, and crushing leftovers increase the surface area. This will speed up the decomposition process. However, too much cutting will cause too much moisture. **Aim for variety in sizes and shapes when preparing leftovers.**

Create and Manage the Pile

"Lasagna Layers" is a simple and effective technique for building and managing compost piles that prevent many problems.

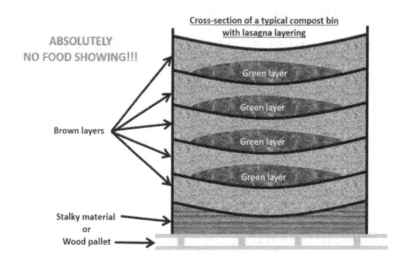

Cross-section of a typical compost bin with lasagna layering

ABSOLUTELY NO FOOD SHOWING!!!

Green layer

Green layer

Green layer

Green layer

Brown layers

Stalky material or Wood pallet

First, use a wood pallet to lift the pile off the ground or fill the bottom of the bin with 6–12 inches of stalky, course material. Next, stuff the container with a substantial nest of brown material. Place your green garbage in the nest's middle. Add one last coat of browns to **completely cover the food**. As compostable are produced and put into the pile, continue to **alternate the layers of brown and green**. The thickness of brown layers ought to be **two or three times** that of green layers.

Turn the pile at least once every year to hasten decay: Then, turn the leftover materials into a new bin using a shovel or pitchfork after first removing the outer layer of browns. Alternately, roll or tumble your trashcan. Add more layers.

Troubleshooting

Even the most seasoned composters occasionally need to troubleshoot an issue. Your chances of averting problems and overcoming obstacles will be significantly improved if you have a solid understanding of the four elements of a composting pile. In the image below are a few of the more typical composting problems:

Issue	Solution
Not heating up	Add greens or larger volumes of browns and greens
Too dry	Add greens or water
Too wet	Add browns or decrease greens
Foul odors	Add more browns
Flies and other pests	Add more browns and no food showing

Utilizing Completed CompostU

The finished compost is crumbly and dark brown. There won't be any compostables that can be identified and there won't be any unpleasant smells. Finished compost can be produced in a year or longer, depending on the materials added and how frequently the pile was turned. Materials made of wood will take longer to decompose. **Be patient; composting does occur**.

Note: Adding ready-made compost to the plot can increase soil fertility.

Ready-made compost can be used in:

1. Mulch or "dress" planting areas.
2. Improve the soil before planting.
3. Or as an ingredient in potting material

To new beds, add two inches of compost, and to existing beds, add one inch of compost annually. As much as possible, integrate the compost into the ground.

CHAPTER 3

A COMPOST PILE'S CARE REQUIREMENTS

Gardeners and farmers utilize compost, an organic combination rich in nutrients, to help develop robust, healthy plants and flowers. Compost piles also offer the additional benefit of recycling many common yard and household waste products that would otherwise end up in landfills, helping to repair depleted soil without costing any additional nutrients. Although the initial decomposition process can take some time, once a compost pile gets rolling, maintaining it is simple. In this Chapter, we'll go over compost pile upkeep.

Steps to Maintain a Compost Pile

1. Create an indentation on the top of the compost pile by arranging it. When the pile starts to look dry, use a garden hose to spray water into the hole. Because the beneficial organisms that allow the compost to degrade properly cannot thrive in a soggy environment, it is crucial to maintain the compost pile moist but not wet.

2. Regular compost turning will ensure optimal air circulation, which promotes the growth of good bacteria and fungi, which accelerates the decomposition process. If you need to hurry things along or if your compost pile smells bad, turn it more frequently.

3. When feasible, shred or otherwise chop materials into tiny bits before adding them to the compost pile. Decomposition will happen faster in smaller fragments.

4. Find out what can be composted. You will be able to produce more compost if you can add more materials to your compost pile. Many kitchen wastes, grass clippings spread out in thin layers, mulched leaves, disease- and pest-free plants as long as they are not weeds, and shredded paper are examples of commonly found materials that can be composted.

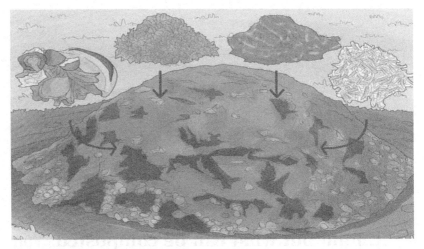

5. If you detect a bad smell, add a straw, pine needles, grass clippings, or plant cuttings. Well-aerate the pile.

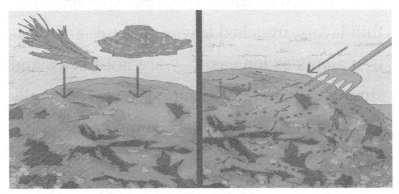

6. If the compost pile is wet, add dry chopped or mulched leaves to absorb the extra moisture. Well-aerate the pile.

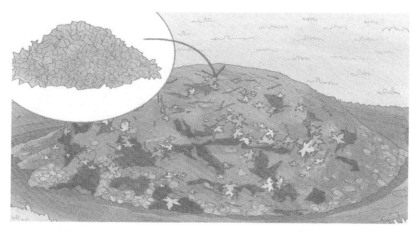

7. Keep a container with a lid and handle in the refrigerator or under the sink. Large pieces of food waste should be chopped or sliced before being placed in the container. Empty the container into the compost pile when it is full. Buy biodegradable compost pail liners that can be thrown in the compost bin as well if you don't routinely produce a lot of kitchen trash to make cleaning the container much simpler.

8. To deter flying insects, cover any exposed produce with 1 to 2 inches (2.5 to 5 cm) of grass clippings.

Tips

1. Your compost pile should not contain any meat, bones, or fish.

2. Compost should be black, crumbly, and earthy smelling when it is finished, not rotten or moldy.

3. In leaf bags or sacks, keep dry leaves close to the compost pile. To assist balance the green components as you add kitchen scraps and other green items, sprinkle a layer of dried

28

leaves on top. The compost pile should be turned anytime new materials are added.

4. Start a second compost pile for the leaves if you have more leaves than your compost bin can manage. With a layer of dirt in between each foot (.3 m) of leaves, the pile should be at least 4 feet (1.2 m) (1.2 m) wide and 3 feet (0.91 m) (.9 m) high. The pile should continue to be damp.

5. To aid hasten the decomposition process, compost activators can be added to your compost pile. In addition to commercial activator treatments, well-rotted chicken manure, young weeds, and grass clippings can also be used.

6. The soil should be amended with compost. It won't take the place of soil.

7. The compost pile is probably too small if it is moist and barely warm in the center. More compost should be added.

8. Never include pet manure in compost that will be applied to edible produce.

9. Weeds and unhealthy plants shouldn't be composted because the compost's addition to the soil can spread them to other planting sites.

What You Will Need

1. Hose for garden

2. Pitchfork

3. Container with a lid and handle for composting kitchen garbage

Heating Compost Piles

Compost production and heat go hand in hand. Temperatures must stay between 90 and 140 degrees F (32-60 C.) for compost microorganisms to be fully activated. Seeds and prospective weeds will also be destroyed by heat. Compost will form more quickly if the right temperature is maintained.

If the temperature of the compost does not rise to the right levels, it will either smell bad or take a very long time to decompose. Compost heating is a typical issue that may be solved with ease.

Tips on Heating Compost

Compost may be heated easily if it has nitrogen, moisture, microorganisms, and mass.

1. Cell development in organisms that support breakdown requires **Nitrogen**. Heat is a byproduct of this cycle. The **absence of "green" material is the most likely cause** when compost pile heating up is a problem. Make sure the ratio of brown to green is roughly 4 to 1. This entails a ratio of four parts dry brown material (such as leaves and shredded paper) to one part green material (such as grass clippings and vegetable leftovers).

2. Compost needs moisture to become active. An overly dry compost pile won't break down. There won't be any heat because there are no bacteria present. Ensure that your pile has enough moisture. Squeezing your palm into the pile is the simplest way to determine this. It must have the texture of a slightly moist sponge.

3. It's also possible that the **bacteria needed** to begin decomposing and heating up in your compost pile are **simply absent**. Throw some dirt onto your compost pile and stir it around with a shovel. The bacteria in the dirt will grow and begin assisting the compost pile's materials in decomposing, which will cause the compost pile to heat up.

4. Last but not least, if your **compost pile is too tiny**, that may be the cause of the compost not heating up. The perfect pile height is from 4-6 feet (1-2 m). Throughout the season, turn your pile once or twice with a pitchfork to ensure that adequate air gets to the core.

Heating compost piles shouldn't be an issue if you're making one for the first time as long as you carefully follow the instructions until you get the hang of the procedure.

CHAPTER 4

HOW TO MAINTAIN COMPOST DURING THE WINTER

Even in the chilly, dark days of winter, a healthy compost pile needs to be maintained year-round. As a result of the lower temperatures, while composting over the winter, the decomposition process does slow down a bit, but bacteria, molds, and mites all survive and require energy to function. Composting in the winter involves some preparation but is a feasible task for most gardeners. To discover more about composting in the winter, continue reading.

Tips for Composting During the winter

Before the arrival of winter, it is recommended to empty compost bins of all useful compost. Compost can be used in raised beds, around the garden, or it can be transferred to a dry container with a lid for use in the spring. Before starting your winter compost heap, harvest the compost to make room for new compost.

If you reside in a location with severe winter weather and brisk winds, keeping the trash can warm is crucial. Place hay or straw bales or leaf bags all around your trash can. This will guarantee that all of the beneficial organisms in the compost will remain warm throughout the winter.

Handling Compost during the Winter

The same principles for managing your compost pile throughout the winter, with layers of browns and greens, apply as always. The greatest compost heaps combine green trash from the kitchen and garden with brown materials like straw, newspaper, and fallen leaves. The only distinction is that you don't have to turn the pile as often while composting in the winter. It is preferable to avoid stirring the winter compost heap too frequently because doing so could cause heat to escape.

Reduce the size of your compost pieces because the cold weather slows down decomposition. Before putting food wastes in the winter compost bin, chop them up, and use a lawnmower to shred the leaves before adding them to the pile. Maintain a damp but not soggy pile. The pile can be extremely soggy in the spring, particularly if it has frozen during the winter. Adding extra browns to absorb the water is a smart technique to control excess moisture.

Winter Composting Tip: Keep a compost bucket with a tight-fitting lid in your kitchen or outside your back door to reduce the number of journeys you need to make in the frigid weather to the compost pile. By the time scraps get to the main compost pile, with good layering, there should be very little smell and they will already be partially decomposed.

CHAPTER 5

MAKING COMPOST INDOORS: HOME COMPOSTING INSTRUCTIONS

Most people in this day and age are aware of the advantages of composting. By recycling food and yard waste through composting, we can prevent our landfills from becoming overflowing. Can you compost indoors? When you think of composting, an outside bin often comes to mind. Of course! Anyone can compost almost any place.

Making Compost at Home

Interesting, huh? The issue at hand is how to compost at home. It's extremely easy. To make compost inside, you must first select a composting container or bioreactor. Since these containers are much smaller than the outdoor bins, they must be carefully planned to create the ideal environment for aerobic heat production that breaks down food waste.

When composting inside, the bioreactor needs to have enough moisture, heat retention, and airflow to allow your organic waste to break down. There are a few straightforward bioreactors that can be used to create compost indoors. When composting indoors, a worm bin or a 20-gallon waste can bioreactor can be used to produce completed compost in two to three months.

For example, an apartment dweller might benefit greatly from indoor composting with worms. Microorganisms and redworms are responsible for decomposition. Vermicomposting does not reach as high of temperatures as other bioreactors. Your apartment's indoor plants can be fertilized using the worm castings that are produced. It's astonishing how quickly these little fellas can transform your undesirable leftovers into top-notch compost since they work so hard. Kids enjoy learning about this, and many schools have vermicomposting programs. Vermicomposting supplies are available online and in many garden centers.

Additional Details about Composting Indoors

You might be wondering what to put in your bioreactor or worm bin now that you have one. All food leftovers may be composted, except for bones, meat, and greasy fats. As a result of the unappealing aroma and potential for rodent attraction, meaty products are never put in the compost. Throw your used coffee and tea bags in there, but leave out the dairy for the same reason as meat.

Additionally, you can utilize the compost or worm bin to dispose of expired cut flowers or other plant debris. To speed up the decomposition process, try to keep the sizes of the items you throw in the compost close to the same. In other words, avoid adding an entire acorn squash to a pot that is primarily filled with coffee grounds and cucumber peels and then asking why it isn't breaking down.

Turn the compost pile occasionally to keep it aerated, which will speed up the decomposition process. By accelerating decomposition, turning the interior compost will also lessen the possibility that the neighbors in 2B will smell something foul.

Okay, go ahead and do it knowing that you are saving one orange rind at a time to help save the world.

CHAPTER 6

TIP FOR PICKING THE IDEAL COMPOST BIN

By converting garbage into something useful, composting is a great way to cut down on kitchen and yard waste. You have what it takes to compost if your yard contains any kind of green trash. Compost minimizes your rubbish by hundreds of pounds annually and replenishes vital nutrients in the soil. Several retail locations sell compost bins for the house, however, if you want to save some money, you can create your compost bin.

Let's look at some of the most popular compost bins for the home to help individuals who are just starting to choose the ideal one:

1. A **Basic Composter** is a self-contained container with a cover to keep your compost organized. These composters are ideal for urban residents or those with little yards.

2. With the turn of a handle, **Spinning Composters** allow you to maintain the rotation of your compost. Although they are slightly more expensive than basic ones, spinning composters typically cook the compost more quickly.

3. A tiny **Kitchen (Indoor) Composter** is perfect for people who either don't have the space outside or aren't interested in an outside compost operation. Beneficial bacteria are used in indoor composters that operate without power. This useful little gadget converts kitchen trash into compost within two weeks.

4. Worm Composter: Worms are excellent at converting waste into usable organic material. Worm composters are standalone devices that can be challenging to use at first. Once you and your worms, however, agree, there is no stopping them.

5. An **Electric "Hot" Composter** is a fantastic choice if money is no object. These contemporary appliances, which can manage up to 5 pounds (2.5 kg) of food every day, are perfectly at home in today's gourmet kitchen. You can obtain compost for your garden that is high in nitrogen in just two weeks. This type accepts everything, including meat, dairy, and fish, and converts them into compost within two weeks, in contrast to other composters that have restrictions on what you can put in.

6. Homemade Compost Bin: You can build a homemade compost bin out of practically any material, including cinder blocks, scrap wood, old wooden pallets, and chicken wire. Online, many websites offer free compost bin plans. Even better, you can create your spinning compost container from 208-liter (55-gallon) plastic drums. If you are creative, there are no limits to what you may design. Even though a homemade compost bin needs some work, it is typically less expensive over time than store-bought containers.

The compost bins that match your space requirements, fall within your price range, and fulfill your needs are the best. Before selecting the ideal compost bin for your requirements, make sure to read all the reviews and conduct some research.

CHAPTER 7

STORING COMPOST

A compost is a living creature that contains microorganisms and bacteria that need air, moisture, and food to survive. Composting is simple to learn how to implement, and if stored on the ground, it can contain more nutrients. You can also store your compost in a compost bin if you are producing it at such high rates that you cannot utilize it right away. Compost storage requires careful moisture management because it can grow mold if it is too wet, but it also shouldn't dry out completely.

How to Store Completed Compost

Every competent gardener has plans. This could imply that your compost is done before it is time to lay it for the following year. That implies keeping the compost in a state where it is still moist and nutrient-rich for the following season is necessary.

One of the simplest ways to store compost is on the ground and covered with plastic sheeting or a tarp. This will stop snow and rain from accumulating on the pile and causing it to become overly wet, but it will still let some humidity leak in and keep it damp. The possibility of worms entering the pile and leaving their valuable castings behind will be a bonus.

Space is a key factor when deciding how to store completed compost. Composting on the ground looks bad and takes up garden space, which many home gardeners lack. You can utilize your compost bin and maintain the compost moderately moistly and rotated, but since many of us always have a batch of compost in the making, the bin is necessary for the upcoming crop of rich soil amendment.

In this situation, you have two options for storing the compost: in plastic bags or inexpensive trash cans. Check the compost's moisture content and give it a good stir to raise the moist bottom layer to the upper, drier layer for the greatest results. Turn the batch with a garden fork. Lightly mix the compost and if it is completely dry.

How to Keep Compost Tea

Fresh Compost tea is one of the simplest fertilizers for an organic gardener to employ. It not only enriches the soil's fertility but also deters some pests and insects. For up to four to six days, compost tea can be kept in a sealed, light-proof container. A bubbler stone or aquarium pump will need to be used to give aeration if you need to store it for a longer period. Compost tea storage will guarantee a supply of active, advantageous bacteria and organisms to enhance the health of your plants.

The Duration of Compost Storage

The optimal time to use compost is right away. The likelihood of losing nutrients increases with storage time. Although it can be kept for the following season, compost must be used before then. If you plan to preserve the compost for a longer period, you can also add extra "food" to the pile or combine it with compost that is nearly done. Increasing the number of organisms will keep the compost alive.

CHAPTER 8

ENHANCING BACTERIA FOR COMPOST

Every living environment on Earth has bacteria, and they are crucial to composting. In actuality, there wouldn't be any compost or even life on earth without compost bacteria. Garden compost contains helpful bacteria that work as the earth's garbage collectors, collecting rubbish and turning it into something useful.

Whereas other living forms perish in harsh environments, bacteria can. Compost naturally occurs in settings like forests where bacteria that promote compost break down organic material like animal and tree droppings. An eco-friendly activity that is well worth the effort is using helpful bacteria in the home garden.

What Compost Bacteria Do

Garden compost contains helpful bacteria that are actively consuming matter to produce heat and carbon dioxide. These heat-loving microbes cause the compost to reach temperatures of up to 140 degrees Fahrenheit (60 degrees Celsius). Bacteria that promote composting are always at work, in all kinds of circumstances, breaking down organic matter.

This rich organic soil is utilized in the garden to improve the soil there and the general health of the plants grown there once it has decomposed.

What Kind of Microorganisms Are in Compost?

You may be curious, what type of bacteria are present in compost? when discussing compost bacteria. Well, there are many different types of bacteria in compost piles (far too many to list), and each one requires a particular environment and a particular kind of organic material to function. Several of the more typical compost microorganisms are as follows:

1. There are microorganisms known as **psychrophiles** that can withstand frigid temperatures and continue to function.

2. Warmer temperatures between 70 and 90 degrees F (21-32 C.) are ideal for **mesophiles**.

55

These bacteria are referred to as aerobic workhorses since they contribute most to breakdown.

3. Thermophiles take control of the compost piles when the temperature rises above 10 degrees F (37 C). The temperature in the pile is raised by **thermophilic bacteria** to a level that destroys any potential weed seeds.

Assisting the Bacteria in the Compost Piles

By adding the correct components to our compost heaps and turning our pile frequently to boost oxygen, which supports decomposition, we can aid microorganisms in compost piles. While compost-enhancing bacteria in our compost pile do most of the work for us, we still need to be careful when building and maintaining our pile to create the optimal circumstances for them to function.

The bacteria present in yard compost will be extremely happy with a nice balance of browns and greens and sufficient aeration, which will hasten the composting process.

CHAPTER 9

COMPOSTING GREEN AND BROWN

Compost Banana Peels (Green)

Many people are delighted to discover that they can use banana peels as fertilizer. Using banana peels in your compost is a great way to include organic matter and some very important nutrients in your compost mix. Learning how to compost banana peels is simple, but there are a few things to keep in mind when composting bananas.

Banana's Effect on Soil Compost

Adding banana peels to your compost pile will help add calcium, magnesium, sulfur, phosphates, potassium, and sodium, which are important for the healthy growth of both flowering and fruiting plants. Bananas in compost also help include healthy organic matter, which helps the compost retain water and lighten the soil when included in your garden.

Additionally, banana peels will break down quickly in compost, letting them include these vital nutrients to compost much faster than other composting materials.

Composting Banana Peels

Composting banana peels is as easy as simply tossing your banana peels into the compost. You can throw them away whole, but be mindful that they may take slower to compost this way. You can haste up the composting process by cutting banana peels into smaller pieces.

59

Many people also marvel if banana peels can be used as direct fertilizer. While, yes, you can use banana peels as fertilizer and it won't damage your plant, it's best to have them composted first. Burying banana peels in the soil under a plant can slow down the procedure that decomposes the peels and makes nutrients available to the plant. This procedure requires air to take place, and buried banana peels will break down much more slowly than those positioned in a properly maintained compost pile that is turned and aired regularly.

So the next time you're enjoying a healthy banana snack, remember that your compost pile (and ultimately your garden) would appreciate some leftover banana peels.

Tomato Plants Composting: When to Compost Tomatoes (Green)

There has always been much debate among gardeners and gardening professionals about the question, "Is it good to compost tomatoes?" or, more precisely, spent tomato plants. Let's take a look at some arguments against composting tomato plants and a discussion of the best way to compost your tomato plants if you choose.

Is It Adequate to Compost Tomatoes?

Once the gardening season is over, there may be many old tomato plants left. Many gardeners believe it is necessary to return plants to the soil through composting. Others think it's too risky when it comes to the potential spread of disease. Here are some reasons why many gardeners choose not to compost tomato plants:

1. Composting might not kill all the seeds: The composting process might not kill all the tomato seeds left on the plant. This could lead to tomato plants appearing in random places in your garden.

2. Composting increases the spread of disease: Tomato plants in compost can spread diseases that could affect next year's garden. Many diseases, such as **fusarium wilt** and **bacterial canker**, can endure the composting process, making them uninvited guests later.

3. Incomplete decomposition: Placing large tomato plants in compost piles can also be a problem, especially if the pile is not managed appropriately. The vines may not decompose correctly, generating an eyesore and mess in the spring when it's time to apply compost.

What Time is best to Compost Tomatoes

Now that you have some of the details about not composting tomato plants, you might be wondering about the right times to compost tomatoes, if at all. The answer here is, yes.

Tomato plants can be composted by gardeners as long as the plants do not have bacterial or fungal diseases. Wilt virus and the curly top virus will not survive long on a dead tomato plant, so plants with these viruses can be composted.

It is also best to break the dead plant material into smaller pieces before including it in the compost pile. Proper management of compost piles is necessary to destroy the plants that have been consumed.

Tomato Plants Composting

For a compost pile to do its job, it must be properly layered, kept moist, and have a constant internal temperature of at least 135 degrees F. (57 C.).

The base layer of any compost pile should be an organic material such as garden waste, clippings, small twigs, etc. The second layer should be the manure of animals, fertilizers, or starters, which will increase the internal temperature. The top layer should be a layer of soil that will introduce advantageous

64

microorganisms into the pile. When the temperature drops below 110 degrees Fahrenheit (43 C.), turn the pile. Turning facilitates the breakdown by mixing the material and introducing air.

Composting Tea Bags (Green)

It's comforting to know that the "dregs" from our regular coffee or tea consumption may also be enjoyed by our gardens. Let's find out more about how using tea bags can help plants thrive.

Can I Place Tea Bags in the Garden?

Tea bags can be put in the garden, without a doubt, but with some limitations. The rate at which your compost pile decomposes is accelerated by adding moist tea leaves to the container.

To determine whether tea bags are compostable before using them as fertilizer, whether in a compost bin or directly around plants, first try to determine if the bag itself is made of 20 to 30 percent polypropylene, which will not break down. These tea bags could have a heat-sealed edge and feel slick to the touch. If so, cut open the bag and throw it away (sorry) while saving the damp tea leaves for composting.

When composting tea bags, you can throw them in the pile without worrying about the composition of the bag and then remove them later if you're feeling very lazy. To each his or her own, but it seems like an extra step to me. If the bag is compostable, it will be abundantly clear because worms and other microbes won't decompose it. Compostable tea bags can be constructed of muslin, silk, or paper.

How to Fertilize Plants Using Tea Bags

Both loose-leaf teas and compostable tea bags can be buried near plants in addition to being decomposed as fertilizer in the compost bin. By adding that nitrogen-rich component, using tea bags in compost balances the carbon-rich components. To use tea bags in compost, you'll need the following things:

1. Leaves of tea (either loose or in bags)
2. A compost container
3. A 3-tined cultivator

After steeping each additional cup or pot of tea, add the cooled tea bags or leaves to the compost bucket where you keep food scraps until you're ready to place them in an outdoor composting area or bin. Following that, the bucket should be emptied into the compost area or, if using a worm bin for composting, emptied into and loosely covered. Pretty basic.

Bury loose tea leaves or tea bags around plants if you want to use them for plant growth right near the root system. Tea bags can be utilized for plant growth because they aid in moisture retention, control weed growth, and provide food for the plant when the tea bag breaks down.

The advantage of using tea bags in compost is that since so many people have strong tea habits and must consume the beverage frequently, a lot of compost can be produced. While caffeine is present, composted tea bags and coffee grounds don't seem to hurt plants or dramatically raise soil acidity.

Tea bags can be composted as an environmentally friendly way to dispose of them which is also great for the health of all your plants. Composting tea bags encourages earthworms, boosts oxygen levels in the soil, maintains soil structure for a more attractive garden, and provides organic matter to improve drainage while maintaining moisture.

Compost Onion Peelings (Green)

Composting is a fantastic process that turns organic waste into useful plant nourishment and soil amendment for gardens. As long as it isn't radioactive or infected, almost any organic waste can be added to the compost pile. Only a few limitations apply, though, and even those may only need to be properly pre-treated before being added to your compost.

Consider potatoes as an example; experts advise against adding them to the pile. In this case, the cause is the potatoes' drive to increase in size and number so that they resemble a mass of tubers rather than an organic combination. Crushing the tubers before including them to the mound will address this problem. But what about composted onions? Can onions be composted? That's a resounding "**yes**" in response. Composting onion waste produces a useful organic product, with a few limitations.

Composting Onion Peelings

Onions have a problem when composted because they want to grow, much like potatoes do. Again, cut it into halves and quarters before putting it in the compost bin to prevent new shoots from emerging from the onions in compost piles.

How to compost onion peelings may be the question you have if you are not trying to compost an entire onion. Although onion skins

71

and scraps do not encourage the growth of additional onions, they may give the pile a bad smell and attract pests or wildlife (or the family dog to dig!). Onions that are rotting do smell horrible.

When composting onions, bury them at least 10 inches (25.5 cm) deep or deeper. You should also be aware that when you turn your compost pile, the smell of rotting onions may briefly make you pause. Onions often take longer to decompose the larger they are when added to the compost. Of course, this rule applies to all major organic leftovers, including branches and sticks as well as vegetables and fruits.

Adding crushed oyster shells, newsprint, or cardboard can also help to eliminate or at the very least minimize offensive odors if the odor is the main concern.

One Final Thought on Composting Onions

Last but not least, composting onions have no impact on the bacteria already present in your compost, maybe only your sense of smell. Onions, on the other hand, should **NOT** be added to bins used for **vermicomposting**. Worms do not care for pungent food scraps and will turn their noses up at onions, broccoli, potatoes, and garlic. Worm gastric systems do not like the high acidity of composted onion waste.

Making Use of Sawdust in Your Compost Pile (Brown)

The majority of individuals who maintain a compost pile are aware of the common items you can add to it. Weeds, leftover food, leaves, and grass clippings are a few examples of these things. How about a few of the odd stuff, though? Things that might not originate from your kitchen or garden? The likes of sawdust.

Making Use of Sawdust in Compost

Woodworking is a common hobby these days (though not as popular as gardening). Many individuals enjoy assembling things by hand and the sense of achievement that comes from taking a bunch of wood planks and transforming them into something beautiful and functional. A lot of sawdust is another byproduct of a woodworking pastime, in addition to a sense of pride. I suppose it seems sensible to wonder, "Can I compost sawdust?" because vegetation, especially trees, make fantastic compost. The quick answer is that any form of sawdust can be composted.

Sawdust would be regarded as a "**brown**" composting material to compost. It is used to balance the nitrogen from the "**green**" composting materials (like food) and to provide carbon to the mixture.

Instruction for Composting Sawdust

When composting sawdust, you should handle it the same way you would dry leaves, which is to say, you should add it in a ratio of roughly 4:1 of brown to green materials.

Adding sawdust to your compost pile is a great way to improve it since it will add a filler that is relatively absorbent and will draw up moisture from the rain and juices from the green material, all of which speed up the composting process.

The type of wood your sawdust is made of is irrelevant here. You can utilize sawdust from any kind of tree, whether it is soft or hard, in your compost pile.

One consideration is whether you plan to compost sawdust from **chemically treated**

wood. Then, before using the compost in your vegetable garden, you should take a few extra precautions to make sure that these pollutants have a chance to leave the compost. The best method to accomplish this is to simply add a few extra watering to your compost pile throughout the summer. This should help leach any dangerous chemicals out of your compost pile combined with regular rainfall and will dilute the toxins being leeched out to levels that won't hurt the surrounding region.

Sawdust can be composted to recover some of its value from what would otherwise be garbage. Consider it as using one hobby to support another.

Utilizing Newspaper as Compost (Brown)

Can I compost the newspaper? This is a question you might have if you get a daily, weekly, or even occasional newspaper. Throwing away so much seems like such a waste. Let's examine whether using the newspaper in your compost pile is permissible and whether there are any issues with doing so.

Can Newspaper Be Composted?

Yes, newspapers are good to put in the compost pile, is the quick answer. Newspaper is a brown composting material that can be used in compost and will help the compost pile add carbon. There are, however, a few considerations to make while composting newspapers.

Instruction for Composting Newspapers

First off, you cannot just throw the newspaper in as bundles when composting it. The first step is to shred the newspapers. Composting successfully requires oxygen. Instead of transforming into rich, brown compost due to lack of oxygen, a bundle of newspapers will instead become a moldy, unappealing mess.

When utilizing newspaper in a compost pile, it's also crucial to maintain an even distribution of browns and greens. Newspapers must be balanced out with green compostable material because they are a brown compostable substance. Make careful to add the shredded newspaper to your compost pile in equal parts with the green compost material.

The impact of newspaper inks on compost piles is another issue that worries a lot of people. Today's newspaper's ink is completely non-toxic. Both color and black and white inks fall under this category. You won't get hurt by the newspaper ink in a compost pile.

You won't have any issues composting newspapers if you bear all of these points in mind. These newspapers can be used to your compost to keep your garden lush and the landfill from getting too full.

Types of Hair for Composting When Adding Hair (Brown)

Composting is a free method of transforming garbage and garden waste into a product that feeds plants while improving soil, as many good gardeners are aware. Many materials can be composted, but a common query is "Can you compost hair?"

Is Hair Compostable?

Compost is essentially organic material that has decomposed into its simplest constituent parts. Compost provides the soil with essential nutrients when it is added to garden soil. In sandy soil, it will aid in water retention, while in dense clay soil, it will improve drainage.

Compost is made by layering green or moist ingredients with brown or dry ingredients, burying them in soil, and then adding water. Together, the chemicals from each sort of substance decompose everything into a single brown mass rich in nutrients. It's crucial to have the appropriate ratios of greens and browns.

So, is hair compostable? Kitchen garbage, recently cut grass, picked weeds, and **yes**, even human hair are examples of "green" materials. In reality, the green components are perfectly willing to consume almost any organic substance that hasn't dried out and isn't an animal's internal organ. These enrich the compost, which in turn enriches the soil, with nitrogen.

Shredded newspaper, dried leaves, and twigs are among the items used to make brown compost. Brown components break down and release carbon into the mixture.

Hair Types for Composting

Don't just add your family's hairbrush bristles to the compost pile. Consult any nearby hairdressers for information. Many of them are accustomed to giving gardeners bags of hair in exchange for animal deterrents and composting materials.

If there is a dog groomer in your neighborhood, offer to take the dog hair off of her hands so you may add extra nitrogen to your compost pile. All hair behaves the same way. You can also use cat hair.

Composting Hair

It's easy to include hair into compost by simply sprinkling it on top of the other green elements when you add the top layer. Spreading the hair out rather than dropping it in big clumps will make it simpler for it to decompose.

It could be beneficial to cover the compost pile with a tarp to hasten the decomposition process. This will aid in keeping the heat and moisture that are required for the decomposition of these components. To mix everything and keep it aerated, turn the compost several times per week.

Composting hair typically needs approximately a month to decompose enough before being added to plant soil.

Pine Needles for Compost (Brown)

Pine needles are an excellent source of organic matter for the garden because they are plentiful and free in most areas of the country. Pine needles offer vital nutrients and enhance the soil's capacity to retain moisture whether they are added to compost or used as mulch around plants. You won't have to worry about any negative impacts if you understand how to compost pine needles.

Pine needles: Are They Bad for Compost?

Because they believe it will increase the compost's acidity, many individuals avoid adding pine needles to their compost. Pine needles have a pH between 3.2 and 3.8 when they fall from the tree, but after composting, they have an almost neutral pH. Pine needles can be added to compost without risk of the final result harming your plants or acidifying the soil. Without first composting them, adding pine needles to the soil may temporarily reduce its pH.

Pine needles break down quite slowly in compost, which is another reason why gardeners steer clear of them. Pine needles have a waxy layer that prevents bacteria and fungi from easily breaking them down. Pine needles' low pH hinders the compost's microbes and slows down the process even more.

The process can be sped up by using aged pine needles, or needles that have been used as mulch for a while; chopped pine needles also decompose more quickly than fresh ones. Create a stack of pine needles, then cut them into pieces by repeatedly running a lawnmower over them. They will break down more quickly the smaller they are.

Pine Needles for Compost

Pine needles don't compact when composted, which is a benefit. As a result, the compost pile becomes hotter and decomposes more quickly. This maintains the pile open so that air may pass through. Pine needles should only make up 10% of the total volume of the compost pile since they decompose more slowly than other organic matter in a compost pile, even when the pile is heated.

Simply leaving pine needles where they fall and letting them act as mulch for the pine tree is an easy and natural approach to composting pine needles. Eventually, they decompose and give the tree rich, organic nutrients. As additional needles drop, the mulch continues to seem new.

Hay Composting: Instructions for Composting Hay Bales (Brown)

Hay has two unique benefits when it is used in compost piles. In the middle of the summer growing season, when the majority of the readily available ingredients are green, it provides you with a ton of brown materials. Hay bale composting also enables you to build an entirely green compost container that finally decomposes into compost. Hay for compost can be purchased from farms that sell damaged hay at the end of the season or from garden retailers that sell seasonal décor. Let's find out more about hay composting.

Composting Hay

Building a square with used hay bales is an easy way to learn how to compost hay. Lay out several bales to form a square outline, then add a layer of bales to reinforce the back and side walls. Put all the compostable items in the square's center. The higher walls help trap in the heat to let the materials rot faster, while the shorter front allows you to reach into the square to shovel and turn the heap once a week.

89

You'll see that some of the walls have started to mix themselves into the composting process once the compost is finished. By cutting the twine holding the bales in place, add the composting hay to the other ingredients. The twine can either be added to the compost pile or saved to be used as natural plant supports for tomato plants. Your supply of compost will grow as a result of the additional hay blending with the original compost.

You should be aware that some farmers use herbicides to control weeds in their hay fields. This won't be a problem if you intend to use the compost for landscaping, but these herbicides harm some food crops.

Grab a trowel full of your finished compost and place it in 20 different locations across the heap, both deep inside and close to the surface, to test it. Combine them all, then combine this mixture in a 2-to-1 ratio with potting soil. Place this combination in one planter and pure potting soil in the other. In each pot, sow three bean seeds. Till the beans have two or three genuine leaves, grow them. The compost is safe for food crops if the plants all have the same appearance. Use this compost exclusively for landscaping if the plants in it are stunted or otherwise harmed.

Discover More about Composting Ash (Brown)

Can ash be used in compost? **Yes**. Ashes can be helpful in the garden, especially in the compost pile, because they don't contain nitrogen and won't burn plants. Compost made from wood ash can be an excellent supplier of potassium, lime, and other trace nutrients.

Compostable Fireplace Ashes

The best approach to using ashes in the garden is to compost them first. Composting fireplace ashes can assist in preserving the compost's neutral condition. Furthermore, it can add nutrients to the soil. More alkaline wood ash can help balance the acidity of the compost pile's decomposing elements.

Nevertheless, using charcoal ashes from grills may not be a wise idea. Because of the additions in the charcoal, compost containing charcoal may have chemical traces. When applied in excessive quantities, these compounds can be damaging to plants. Therefore, it is preferable to stick with wood ash—as long as the wood is natural and untreated.

Composting Wood Ash Instead of Direct Ash Applications

You shouldn't apply ashes directly on plants, especially acid-loving ones like rhododendrons, azaleas, and blueberries, as they tend to elevate the pH of the soil. Wood ash can also stop plants from growing in large amounts by limiting minerals like iron. Apply it indirectly unless a soil test reveals a low pH or potassium level. However, adding wood ash to the compost pile will reduce the likelihood of such problems in the future and can be added to the soil as a safe, balanced fertilizer.

In addition to enhancing soil health, placing wood ash compost around plants may help deter some insect pests, such as slugs and snails. Ashes from your fireplace or campfire can be disposed of in an easy and environmentally responsible way by composting, which can also improve the soil quality in your garden.

CHAPTER 10

MANAGING COMPOSTING ISSUES

Flies in Compost

It makes sense to wonder whether there should be a lot of flies in your compost considering that it is full of rotten vegetable matter, manure, and kitchen scraps. But the reply for this your wondering is yes and no.

Flies in the Compost Bin

If you don't construct your compost pile properly, there can be a lot of flies buzzing around the bin all the time. On the other side, proper compost pile management is the best way to keep houseflies in compost to a minimum as well as a massive way to produce more of that "black gold" for your gardens.

Houseflies are a nuisance, but they can also be harmful to your health and the health of your family because they are known to transfer several human diseases. Maintaining your compost pile will assist stop the spread of flies.

Causes of Houseflies in Compost and Solutions

Compost piles are where most pests and houseflies are found because they are rich in their natural food. To ensure a food supply for their offspring, they lay eggs in the same location after they consume. In a few days, these eggs develop into larva, or maggots, adding to the **"ick factor"** associated with flies. If you neglect your compost pile long enough, the back of your yard might resemble a CSI crime scene.

Managing compost piles is the answer to this issue. Only at the proper temperature and with an abundance of food would compost flies survive. Always bury your green, or wet, elements first, followed by your brown ingredients, and then add soil on top. The flies can't easily access the manure and decaying vegetables if they aren't on the surface of the soil.

By regularly turning the pile, you'll encourage the organisms that break down the pile and heat the interior while also increasing the oxygen in the middle of the pile. To avoid cooler borders and a warmer center, keep the pile level rather than allowing it to pile up in the middle.

Start by turning and then raking the pile each day if you have a fly problem in your compost bin. Do this repeatedly until the larva perish and the flies go. Reduce the turning and raking to twice a week once the issue has been resolved or the air has become significantly cooler. You won't have to exert as much physical labor, but you will still generate enough heat to keep the flies away.

Larva in Compost Piles

You've probably encountered the comparatively unbothered soldier fly larva if you've been disturbed by grayish brown larvae found in compost piles. These grubs flourish in compost piles that include a lot of greenery and extra moisture. Soldier flies in compost are beneficial to the environment even though they may be unsightly to the average gardener. You could do better to educate yourself about soldier flies and all the good they can do rather than attempting to eradicate them as with other compost pests.

Soldier Flies: What Are They?

What are soldier flies? These quite large insects, which resemble black wasps, are completely safe to people and other mammals despite their size. They can't bite you or harm you in any other way because they lack mouths and stingers. This insect spends its fly stage of life flying around, mating, laying eggs, and dying two days later. They favor places that people avoid, including manure dumps and outhouses, avoid houses and help keep the common housefly away.

Finding Soldier Fly Larva in Compost Piles

The soldier fly larva starts to prove their value once they emerge from the eggs. They excel at reducing organic waste and household garbage into a state that is simpler for ordinary worms to ingest.

They reduce the smell and risk of disease transmission in locations where animal waste is stored by breaking down manure in a couple of days. The worms drop away once they have broken down manure piles into their parts, making them simple to collect for use as chicken feed. This larva is a favorite food of birds and a good source of protein.

What should I do with the soldier fly larva? When you realize how beneficial these tiny wigglers are, you'll want to support them in your compost pile. Instead of burying it behind dry leaves, keep the amount of green material, such as kitchen garbage, on the top of the heap. To assist maintain the moisture levels, water the pile a little more frequently than usual.

However, if soldier fly larvae appear to be dominating and displacing the typical earthworms in the compost, start burying kitchen waste beneath at least 4 inches (10 cm) of leaves, paper, and other brown items. You should also reduce the amount of moisture the pile receives.

Worms in Compost Soil

Your compost pile may have a significant number of white, tiny, thread-like worms moving through it if you've added substances that alter the pH balance or if it's been unusually wet due to rain. Contrary to what you would believe, these are not young red wigglers but rather the pot worm, a separate kind of worm. Let's find out more about pot worms in compost.

Pot Worms: What Are They?

Pot worms are just another organism that consumes trash and aerates the soil or compost nearby if you're wondering what they are. Although white worms in compost aren't a direct threat to anything in your bin, they flourish well in environments that the red wigglers find unpleasant.

If pot worms have taken over your compost pile completely and you want to reduce their population, you'll need to alter the compost's conditions. Pot worms in compost indicate that the other helpful worms aren't flourishing as they should, so altering the compost's conditions can alter the worm population.

Pot Worms: Where Do They Come From?

There are worms in all healthy garden soil, but the majority of gardeners only have a basic understanding of the red wiggler worm. So, from where do pot worms come from? Although they were only a small portion of what you observe during an infestation, they were present all along. When the environment is favorable for pot worms, they increase at an alarming rate. Although they won't directly injure any other worms in the compost, common wiggler worms do not enjoy the same level of comfort as pot worms do.

Turn the compost pile periodically, forgo watering for a week or so, and cover it with a tarp when rain threatens to help the pile dry up. After receiving this treatment for a few days, even the dampest compost will start to dry up.

By adding some lime or phosphorus to the pile, you can alter the pH balance of the compost. Add some powdered lime (such as that used to line baseball fields) or eggshells, which have been crushed into a fine powder and sprinkled over the compost, along with some wood ashes. The number of pot worms should start to drop right away.

If you need a quick fix while the other requirements are fulfilled, soak some old bread in milk and place it on the compost pile. The bread will become covered in worms, which can be picked off and thrown away.

Bugs and Animals in Compost

Composting is an awesome way to use yard trash and kitchen scraps in your garden. Compost is a valuable source of organic matter for plants and is rich in nutrients. While composting is very simple, insect control in compost piles calls for forethought planning and effective compost pile management.

Should I Expect Bugs in My Compost Bin?

Should my compost bin have bugs? This is a common question. You are probably going to have some pests if you have a compost pile. Insects can breed in your compost pile if it is not built properly or if you don't stir it often enough. Common pests in compost include the following:

1. In contrast to house flies, **stable flies** have a needle-like beak that protrudes from the front of their heads. Wet straw, heaps of grass clippings, and straw mixed with manure are all popular places for stable flies to deposit their eggs.

2. Approximately one inch (2.5 cm) long, **green June beetles** are metallic green bugs. These beetles put their eggs in decomposable material.

3. Common **houseflies** also like moist decomposing stuff. They favor manure and decaying trash, but you may also find them in other organic debris like composted grass clippings.

It's not necessarily a bad thing to have some bugs in compost, but they can get out of control. To help the pile dry out, try increasing your brown content and adding some bone meal. Spraying an orange-colored solution around your compost pile appears to help control the fly population.

Animal Pests in Compost Bins

You might have an issue with raccoons, rodents, or even domestic animals getting into your compost pile depending on where you reside. For many animals, compost serves as a desirable food source and home. All compost owners should be aware of the best practices for keeping animals out of the compost pile.

Animals won't be as drawn to your compost if you manage your pile effectively by rotating it frequently and maintaining a nice brown-to-green ratio.

Keep any meat or by-products of meat away from the pile. Additionally, avoid adding any leftovers that contain oil, cheese, or seasonings to the pile because these ingredients all attract rodents. Make sure not to compost any cat litter or animal waste from non-vegetarian pets.

Maintaining your trash can away from anything that could serve as a natural food source for an animal is another strategy of prevention. Bird feeders, pet food dishes, and berry-bearing trees all fall under this category.

Another strategy to maybe deter animal pests is to line your compost container with wire mesh.

If Possible Use a Closed Compost Bin System

Knowing the kind of compost system you have will help you prevent animals from getting into the compost pile. Open compost bin systems can be quite effective for certain people, but they are frequently more challenging to maintain than an enclosed system. Animal pests can be repelled with the aid of a closed bin system with ventilation. Even though some pests will crawl beneath a bin, a closed system is too much labor for most animals and also helps to control odor.

Fix Compost That Smells Bad

Although compost is great for the garden, a compost pile occasionally gets a little smelly. Because of this, a lot of gardeners are curious as to why compost smells. A more pressing question is "How to stop compost from stinking." You have options if your compost stinks.

Do Compost Smell?

It shouldn't smell terrible if the compost pile is balanced appropriately. If your compost pile does not adequately heat up and break down the organic material, it will not smell like dirt and there is a problem.

Only when you are composting manure in your compost pile is there an exception to this rule. Commonly, this will smell until the manure decomposes. You can cover the pile with 6-12 inches (15-30 cm) of straw, leaves, or newspaper to mask the smell of composting manure. This will significantly lessen the smell of composting manure.

How Come Compost Smell?

If your compost smells unpleasant, your compost pile's equilibrium may be out of whack. Composting is a series of actions that are intended to accelerate the breakdown of organic waste and, as a byproduct, keep the compost from smelling foul.

A compost pile can smell foul for a variety of reasons, including having too many greens (nitrogen material), not being mixed well, not having enough aeration, and having too much moisture.

Get Rid of Compost Smell

To truly stop your compost from smelling, you must address the root cause of the odor. Here are some solutions to some typical problems.

1. A **surplus of green materials.** The smell of sewage or ammonia will be present in your compost pile if there is too much green waste there. This suggests that the balance of the browns and greens in your compost is off. Adding brown materials like leaves,

newspaper, and straw will assist in restoring balance to your compost pile.

2. The organic material in compost piles must be appropriately aerated with oxygen for effective decomposition. The compost will begin to smell if your pile is **compacted**. Too little aeration will cause the compost to smell bad or rotten. Turn the compost pile to help the compost absorb air and eliminate odors. To prevent the pile from over-compacting once more, you could also wish to add additional "fluffy" materials like dried leaves or dry grass.

3. Too much moisture. A gardener may frequently find that their compost smells in the spring. This is because the compost pile is overly saturated as a result of all the rain. A compost pile that becomes very damp won't have adequate airflow, and the result will be the same as if the pile had been compacted. Too-wet compost may smell bad or like rotten eggs and will appear slimy, especially if it contains green material. Turn the compost and add some dry brown pieces to absorb some of the moisture to address this source of a smelly compost pile.

4. Layering. A compost pile occasionally contains the ideal ratio of green and brown material, but these items were added to the pile in layers. If the green material is kept separate from the brown stuff, it will begin to break down improperly and emit an unpleasant odor. The compost pile will smell like sewage or ammonia if this happens. Simply improving the pile's mixing will resolve this.

It will help keep your compost pile from smelling if you take proper care of it, such as turning it frequently and maintaining a balance between your greens and browns.

Maintain an Odorless Compost Bin

Compost is a cheap and reusable soil amendment. It is simple to create in the backyard using plant material and discarded cooking scraps. However, maintaining an odorless compost bin requires some work. The nitrogen and carbon content of the compost must be balanced, and the pile must be kept fairly moist and aerated, to control odors.

What causes compost piles to smell? Small animals like snails and worms, as well as bacteria and other microorganisms, aid in the breakdown of organic waste. For all of this life to exist and break down the substance, oxygen is necessary. A smell-free compost bin also requires a proper nitrogen and carbon balance. Another element is moisture, and some foods, like meat, should be avoided since they take longer to compost and can leave harmful bacteria in the finished product.

Taking Care of Compost Odors

Anything that formerly contained life can be composted. Meat and bones take longer and shouldn't be added unless you are an expert. The material, water, oxygen, and heat are the four key components in composting. Compost piles may smell if these four components are not carefully balanced.

About one-quarter of the pile's contents should be nitrogen-rich, and the other three-quarters should be carbon-rich. Make sure your compost heap is appropriately balanced with greens and browns because carbon-rich materials are often brown while nitrogen-rich products are typically green. Sources of nitrogen include:

1. Lawn cuttings
2. Kitchen waste

Among the carbon sources are:

3. Tattered Newspaper
4. Straw
5. Leaf litter

The pile must always be kept moist but never waterlogged. By constantly turning the pile, the bacteria and organisms that are doing all the work are exposed to oxygen. For optimal decomposition, compost has to reach temperatures of 100 to 140 degrees Fahrenheit

(37-60 C). Using a black bin or covering a pile with dark plastic will raise the temperature.

This careful balancing of organic content and conditions controls odor in compost. Odors may develop if one component of the cycle is unstable, which throws the entire process off. For instance, the heat-loving microbes—which are in charge of the initial breakdown of the material—will not be present if the compost is not warm enough. That implies that the materials will just sit there and rot, producing unpleasant odors.

During the aerobic respiration process, the bacteria and other creatures that decompose the material release carbon dioxide and heat. This increases solar heat and promotes more bacteria and microorganisms for composting which happens more quickly. Since smaller parts compost more quickly, odors are diminished. Food leftovers should be chopped up into little bits, and woody debris should only be 1/4 inch (.6 cm) in diameter.

Fixing Smelly Compost Piles

Ammonia or sulfur odors are warning signs of an imbalanced pile or poor conditions. If the pile is excessively wet, check to see if you need to add dry dirt to fix it.

1. Turn the pile at least once each week to provide the microscopic organisms that are decomposing the waste with oxygen.

2. If you smell ammonia, which indicates too much nitrogen, increases the carbon.

3. To keep it warm enough, place your pile or bin where it will receive direct sunlight.

With the four elements in composting in a properly maintained equilibrium, odor control in compost is simple.

My Compost Tea Smell Bad

Farmers and gardeners have used compost and water to make an extract for hundreds of years to supplement the nutrients in crops. Nowadays, the majority of individuals create brewed compost tea as opposed to extracts. When made properly, teas don't contain the harmful microorganisms that compost extracts do. What happens, though, if your compost tea has a terrible odor?

My Compost Tea Stinks, Help!

If you have stinky compost tea, you may be wondering if it is safe to use it and, more importantly, what might have gone wrong during the production process. Compost tea shouldn't first smell bad; instead, it should have an earthy, yeasty scent. Therefore, if your compost tea smells terrible, something is wrong.

Compost teas can be made in a variety of ways, but they all share three common components: clean compost, inert water, and aeration.

1. Clean compost is suitable when it is created from the yard and grass trimmings, dry leaves, leftover fruits and vegetables, paper goods, and untreated sawdust and wood chips. Castings from worms are also ideal.

2. Use only pure water that is free of pathogens, salt, heavy metals, nitrates, pesticides, and chlorine. Remember that tap water probably contains a lot of chlorine if you use it. Similar to how you would when setting up a fish tank, let it sit for the night.

3. Aeration is crucial for maintaining oxygen levels, which promotes beneficial microbial growth. Other ingredients that you could choose to use include molasses, fish-based products, yeast, kelp, or green plant tissues.

All of the aforementioned components are essential when making compost teas, but there are a few other factors to consider if you want to prevent an unpleasant compost tea odor.

1. The size of the tea bag, whether it be made of silk, burlap, or an old nylon sock, is crucial since you only want soluble components to dissolve in the water. Make sure to make your bag out of untreated material.

2. The right proportion of compost to water should be used. If you use too much water, the tea will become diluted and less effective. Similarly, too much compost and an abundance of nutrients can encourage the growth of bacteria, resulting in anaerobic conditions, oxygen depletions, and unpleasant-smelling compost tea.

3. Another key factor is the mixture's temperature. Cold temperatures will decrease microbial growth, while high temperatures may produce evaporation, which will inhibit the bacteria.

4. Last but not least, the period your compost tea is brewed is crucial. The majority of teas have to be of good quality and utilized within 24 hours. While teas made under less ideal conditions may need to steep for a few days to a few weeks, those that are well-aerated require shorter brew durations.

Can Smelly Compost Tea Be Used?

Don't use your compost if it smells bad. It might even endanger the plants. There's a significant chance that you require improved aeration. These guys stink because hazardous bacteria are growing due to insufficient aeration.

Use most teas within 24 hours as well. It is more likely that harmful microorganisms will begin to proliferate the longer it sits. A concentrated mixture can be made by mixing the right amount of clear water (5 gallons (19 L) and clean compost (one pound (0.5 kg)) before applying it.

Overall, producing compost tea has a lot of advantages, from disease prevention to increasing plants' ability to absorb nutrients, and is well worth the effort, even if you have to do a little experimenting along the way.

Vegetables Are Popping From the Compost Pile

Are seeds growing in compost? I'll admit it. I'm slack. As a result, I frequently notice stray vegetables or other plants in my compost. Even though I just pull them up, some people are more alarmed by this situation and question how to stop seeds from growing in their compost.

Why Do Plants Keep Growing in Compost?

You are composting seeds, or more accurately, you are not composting them, which is the simple explanation for why vegetables are sprouting up in your compost. Either you are among the lazy individuals, like me, who just chuck everything into the compost, or the temperature of your compost is not high enough to prevent the seeds from sprouting.

How to Prevent Sprouts of Vegetables in Compost

Be mindful of the compost pile's dynamics. The compost pile must maintain a temperature of between 130 and 170 degrees Fahrenheit (54 and 76 degrees Celsius) and must be turned frequently if the temperature falls below 100 degrees Fahrenheit (37 C.). The seeds will be destroyed by a properly heated compost pile, but it will take some considerable monitoring and work.

The right amounts of carbon and nitrogen must be present for the compost pile to heat up, in addition to moisture and turning the pile. Brown garbage, like dead leaves, produces carbon, whereas green waste, like grass clippings, produces nitrogen. To ensure that a compost pile can adequately heat up, the general rule of thumb is 2-4 parts carbon to 1 part nitrogen. Turn the pile frequently, breaking up any large bits, and add moisture as necessary.

The pile should also have adequate room for composting to occur successfully. For composting seeds and dying them off, a pile 3 feet (1 m) square (27 cubic feet (8 m)) would do, or a compost container will also work. Build the compost pile all at once, and don't add further material until the mound has dropped. Utilizing a compost crank or a garden fork, turn the pile once every week. Before using the compost in the garden, let it sit for two weeks without turning once the pile has been composted completely. At this point, the material should resemble dark brown soil without any discernible organics.

The temperature of the pile won't ever become hot enough to kill seeds if you are doing "cool composting" (also known as "lazy composting"), which is simply piling up the trash and letting it rot. Then, you can either remove the undesirable plants "ala Moi" or refrain from adding any seeds to the mixture. I must admit that I do refrain from including some adult weeds because I do not want them to spread throughout the yard. Additionally, we don't add "sticker" plants like blackberries to the compost pile.

Can Seedlings from Compost Be Use?

Okay, yeah. Cucumbers, tomatoes, and even pumpkins are among the perfectly edible vegetables that some compost bin "volunteers" produce. Don't remove the stray plants if they don't bother you. Let them grow throughout the season; you never know when you'll be able to gather more fruits or vegetables.

CHAPTER 11

ADVANCE COMPOSTING

Growing Organically Using Mushroom Compost

Compost from mushrooms is a fantastic fertilizer for garden soil. There are numerous methods to go about organic gardening with mushroom compost, and it has several advantages for the garden.

Mushroom Compost: What Is It?

An example of a slow-release organic plant fertilizer is mushroom compost. Mushroom producers create the compost using organic materials including hay, straw, corn cobs, hulls, and horse or poultry manure.

Mushroom compost recipes may occasionally change due to how mushrooms are grown to differ somewhat amongst growers. The compost can also include other materials like gypsum, peat moss, lime, soybean meal, and several other organic materials.

The compost is first steam pasteurized to remove any hazardous chemicals and weed seeds. Then the mushroom spawn is added, and the top of the pile is top-dressed with a mixture of sphagnum moss and lime to promote the growth of mushrooms.

133

The three to four weeks it takes for mushroom composting to complete are meticulously watched by mushroom growers to maintain the right temperatures. The leftover compost is disposed of after the process is finished and sold as fertilizer.

Compost from Mushrooms for Gardening

Typically, mushroom compost is marketed in bags with the labels SMC or SMS (spent mushroom compost or spent mushroom substrate). It can be purchased from many garden centers or landscape supply businesses. Depending on how much is needed for the garden, mushroom compost can also be bought by the truckload or bushel.

The compost made from mushrooms has many applications. Lawns, gardens, and container plants can all benefit from their use as soil amendments. However, due to its high quantities of soluble salt, this product should be taken with caution. These salt concentrations can hurt young seedlings, kill germinating seeds, and affect salt-sensitive plants like azaleas and rhododendrons.

Benefits of Mushroom Composted

However, despite its high salt concentration, mushroom compost has more benefits than disadvantages. A compost of this kind is moderately priced. It provides nutrients for optimal plant growth and improves the soil. Additionally, mushroom compost improves the soil's ability to retain water, requiring less frequent watering.

The majority of garden plants are suitable for mushroom compost. Fruits, vegetables, herbs, and flowers are just a few of the many plant types that it promotes growing. When using mushroom compost in organic gardening, make sure to completely mix it into the soil before planting, or let it sit over the winter and use it in the spring.

Composting Gin Waste

Chaff, seeds, and other plant debris that is not beneficial to the business are left over when cotton is processed. However, it is a naturally occurring material that we can compost to provide a rich source of nutrients to top up the soil. In cotton gins, all extra material is removed, and the harvest is separated from the trash.

Gin waste or these leftovers can produce large levels of nitrogen and minute quantities of phosphate and potassium when composted. Farmers are now able to compost cotton gin waste in three days thanks to recent advancements in composting equipment. Gin waste compost is also created using less complex techniques.

Values of Cotton Gin Waste's Nutrients

Gin garbage compost can produce up to 2.85% nitrogen per 43.66 lbs/ton (21.83 kg/metric ton) when measured in pounds per ton. The contents of the minor macronutrients, potassium and phosphorus, are .2 at 3.94 lb/ton (1.97 kg/metric ton) and .56 at 11.24 lb/ton (5.62 kg/metric ton), respectively.

Given that nitrogen is one of the essential nutrients for plant growth, the nutrient values of cotton gin waste are particularly intriguing. Cotton gin waste is a good soil addition when combined with other composted materials once it has fully decomposed.

Composting Cotton Gin Waste

Industrial composters used by commercial farmers maintain high temperatures and stir the gin waste frequently. These can complete the task in a matter of days, after which it must be spread out in windrows for at least a year to dry.

Gin waste can be composted by people other than farmers. Similar work can be done by the home gardener in a vacant, sunny area of the yard. Create a hill of material that is several feet deep and long and wide. Water should be added to raise the moisture content uniformly to about 60%. Work around the damp portions of the trash with a garden fork while moistening the dry areas. It is always maintained somewhat damp to compost gin waste. To prevent odors and kill weed seeds, turn the pile once a week.

In your gin garbage windrow, take periodic readings with a soil thermometer. Turn the pile once the temperature drops to 80 degrees Fahrenheit (26 degrees Celsius) two inches (5 cm) below the surface.

To maintain the heat in the pile, late-season composting gin waste should be covered with black plastic. Most weed seeds will die if the compost temperature stays at 100 degrees Fahrenheit (37 degrees Celsius) or higher. Pigweed, which is most prevalent in the middle of the United States, is the single exception. After the material has decomposed for a few months, spread the pile out in a layer no thicker than a few inches. This will lessen odor and complete the composting.

Uses for Gin Trash Compost

Because it is light, gin waste compost doesn't spread well unless other organic components are also used. Gin waste can be used in gardens, containers, and even on ornamental plants after being blended with soil, manure, or other compost.

Avoid using the cotton gin garbage on food plants if you can't identify the source of it.

Powerful chemicals are frequently used by cotton farmers; some of these poisons may still be present in the compost. If not, use the compost like any other soil amendment.

Vermicomposting

Want to give your organic waste and food scraps a new purpose? Worms can be able to assist. Vermicomposting is a fantastic way to recycle waste and turn garbage into nutrient-dense soil if you can get past the initial shock of keeping worms as pets. Here is all the information you require to begin using the approach.

Vermicomposting: What is it?

Vermicomposting commonly referred to as worm composting, is the practice of feeding natural material—such as vegetable and fruit peels—to worms, who then consume it and digest it.

They excrete the crumbs in worm castings after they have gone through their digestive system. Before you freak out, consider that those castings are a rich, nutrient-dense substance that can transform soil into a plant's dream environment. (It's frequently called "black gold"!)

Regular Composting Vs Vermicomposting

Similar to composting, vermicomposting aims to transform organic matter into a nutrient-rich soil supplement that you can use in your garden.

The two processes differ in how long they take, how and where they are carried out, and what happens as a result.

Worm compost frequently has a substantially higher nutrient content than conventional compost, which is one of the main benefits of vermicomposting.

Because you must layer the compost pile and turn it frequently, typically once per week, composting also necessitates additional physical work. When the weather changes in the colder months, it might be challenging because it typically needs to be done outside.

Regarding weather and space needs, vermicomposting is more adaptable. Your worm bin can be kept indoors or outdoors, somewhere where the temperature isn't too high or low.

Even if you don't have much space, you can still do it indoors in an apartment. The corner of a room can easily accommodate a worm bin.

Benefits of Composting With Worms

1. It is durable: Vermicomposting is a method of recycling the organic waste as opposed to throwing it out. Finding alternate applications for food waste is crucial because it now makes up around 25% of landfills in the US (where it releases dangerous greenhouse gases).

2. It makes excellent soil: Food and plant waste should be returned to the earth since doing so create a closed-loop system of organic nutrients that is extremely helpful to both plants and microbes.

3. It is fertilizer free of chemicals: The health of the soil and wildlife might be harmed

144

by using chemical fertilizers or pesticides. Worm castings are a secure and organic technique to restore overused or nutrient-depleted soil.

The following simple and inexpensive method can be used to create your vermicomposting bin, or you can purchase one already built.

What is required to assemble a Worm Bin

1. 2 12-inch-deep, dark-colored plastic bins or containers (they shouldn't be clear because worms are light-sensitive) plus one lid.
2. Drill.
3. Small brick or ceramic pot.
4. Bedding (like shredded paper, cardboard, straw, hay, dry leaves, dirt, or wood chips).
5. Your preferred worm.

Assembling Your Trash Can

1. Drill 15 to 20 holes round the top sides of one bin using a drill bit between 3/32" and 3/16". Your worms will get air from these. After that, drill 15 to 20 holes through the bin's bottom. These are there to drain away any potential moisture buildup.

2. Put a small brick or ceramic pot on the floor of the other bin. After that, place the air-holed bin inside of this one. The brick or pot will guarantee that there is room for the trash to gather. You don't want your worms to escape, so there shouldn't be much room between the sides of your containers. The entire process needs to be airtight.

3. Put a lid on the top bin.

4. Fill your top container with 4 to 6 inches of bedding. Your worms can be added once you have prepared the bedding, and they will burrow down into it. The bedding will assist regulate excessive moisture levels, offer protection from extremes, and add necessary air for your worms.

5. You are then prepared to feed!

Picking Your Worms

Even though it could be appealing to search for worms in your backyard on your own, not all worm species are good candidates for composting.

Instead of collecting worms from your yard, buy the right species from a local source. Yes, there are worm suppliers.

The kind of worm you purchase from them will mostly depend on the climate where you live, but these are some worthwhile possibilities to consider:

1. Red wigglers (can live in most weather): One of the most common worms used in vermicomposting is the red wiggler. They are a wonderful option for many areas of the country since they can withstand a wide range of temperatures.

2. The European nightcrawler Worms (have a liking for cooler climates): You might want to choose European nightcrawler worms if you reside in a colder climate. They reproduce more slowly than the red wiggler worms but create larger biomass (finished material)" and "prefer cooler temperatures and are found slightly deeper in the earth."

3. African nightcrawlers and Indian blue worms (have a liking for warmer climates): The Indian blue worm and the African nightcrawler are further options, but they "are more suited to tropical conditions.

The short answer is yes, if you want to mix different worm species in one bin, although there may be restrictions. One kind of worm may come to dominate over time. If one species has superior environmental conditions to another, it will grow more quickly.

Feeding the Worms and Keeping the Container Clean

Simply fill the worm's bin with a mixture of food scraps (green and brown) and "bedding" materials like shredded paper, cardboard, straw, hay, dry leaves, mud, or wood chips to start the process.

One of the most crucial steps in the process is feeding the worms, but you must be careful with what and how much you give them.

Worms can consume a wide range of organic substances, such as leftover fruit and vegetable pieces, coffee grounds, and tea bags. Citrus fruits and peels should be avoided, though, as they are acidic and difficult for worms to digest. Additionally, you shouldn't put any dairy or animal products in the trash can.

Your worms will consume both food scraps and their bedding. You should have a higher content of bedding than food waste since your worm bedding is also food for worms.

Get details on how much food your worms consume when you purchase them. To keep your bed in good condition, pay special attention to how much food and moisture it receives at all times. You'll be able to identify when the system is out of balance relatively fast.

If you overfeed the worms, the extra food will decay and produce an unpleasant odor. Causing rotting and heat accumulation and possibly killing the worms.

Overfeeding can also cause moisture to accumulate. Due to the high water content of the vegetable (80% or more), "you add moisture every time you add food waste."

You should wait on adding more scraps if you find that the worms aren't eating the food or the bin smells unpleasant.

Tips and Tricks

Here, are the top vermicomposting tips for those just getting started:

1. Using a small hand rake, gently loosen the contents of your bin from time to time to let air into the container. By doing this, you can keep your compost bin odor-free and provide your worms access to fresh air (which, fascinatingly enough, they breathe through their skin!).

2. Because the heat from the sun can dry up your worms' vital skin, keep your bin away from direct sunlight. The ideal places for them tend to be dim locations like garages or basements.

3. Put your trash can in the warmest part of your garage or basement during the colder months. Keep the bedding levels high for additional protection from harsh temperatures.

4. Every time, feed the worms somewhere new in the container. By doing this, the worm population is kept from being overly concentrated in one place.

5. Ammonia odor indicates anaerobic decomposition is occurring in the trash can. This suggests that the atmosphere is excessively moist and that your soil may be saturated, which can cause your worms to perish. At this point, draining the bottom bin, adding fresh, dry bedding, and stirring the contents of the bin to add more oxygen are all wise moves.

FAQS

How Frequently Should I Feed The Worms?

Once a week is typically adequate. Make sure you check that they're eating everything you give them.

What Symptoms Indicate An Excess Of Moisture?

Fruit flies/fungus gnats, unpleasant scents, or leached liquid from your bin are indications that there is too much moisture in a worm bin.

Can I Run A Test To Determine The Moisture Content?

Take a handful of the material in your bin and squeeze it to get an idea of the moisture content. Your bin is too damp if water leaks out of the bin material. When you realize your trash can has too much moisture and water, to help absorb some of the moisture, put more dry bedding.

Is Mold In The Trash A Bad Thing?

A tiny quantity of mold is normal and not cause for alarm. However, excessive mold can be a sign of other issues, like overfeeding.

Can I Use Vermicomposting All Year Long?

As long as the weather isn't too chilly for the worms, you can worm compost. Compost production slows down when temps fall below 60 degrees. Your worms may die at temperatures below 40 degrees,"

What Should I Do If Fruit Flies Are Present?

Food that is too much or is starting to rot will attract fruit flies. You want to keep the conditions inside the worm bin from becoming too damp and anaerobic since fruit flies are drawn to fermenting fruits and vegetables.

To make it simple to bury the food waste, put extra bedding in the bin. Don't scatter the scraps on the top. Instead, make room for them to be placed there. Then thoroughly cover them with dirt and wet paper.

How Soon Can The Compost Be Harvested?

Depending on how many worms you have, how quickly they reproduce, and the types of food in your bin, you can harvest after three to six months. Chop scraps into pieces about an inch in size to quicken the process.

Final Thought

Starting a vermicomposting bin is a rewarding way to observe nature at work and get more involved with your environment, even though it does require some trial and error. With this knowledge, you'll soon be gathering your black gold.

Made in the USA
Monee, IL
30 January 2024

52657207R00095